Y0-AGT-577

UNITED IN CAUSE

THE SONS OF LIBERTY

by Don Nardo

Content Adviser: Julie Richter, Ph.D., Lecturer,
Lyon G. Tyler Department of History, College of William & Mary

Reading Adviser: Alexa L. Sandmann, Ed.D., Professor of Literacy,
College and Graduate School of Education, Health,
and Human Services, Kent State University

COMPASS POINT BOOKS
a capstone imprint

Compass Point Books
151 Good Counsel Drive
P.O. Box 669
Mankato, MN 56002-0669

 This book was manufactured with paper containing
at least 10 percent post-consumer waste.

Editor: Brenda Haugen
Designer: Bobbie Nuytten
Media Researcher: Svetlana Zhurkin
Library Consultant: Kathleen Baxter
Production Specialist: Jane Klenk
Cartographer: XNR Productions, Inc.

Library of Congress Cataloging-in-Publication Data
Nardo, Don, 1947–
  United in cause: the Sons of Liberty / by Don Nardo.
      p. cm.—(Taking a stand)
  Includes index.
  ISBN 978-0-7565-4299-3 (library binding)
  1. Sons of Liberty—Juvenile literature. I. Title. II. Series.
  E216.N37 2010
  369'.12—dc22   2009030371

Visit Compass Point Books on the Internet at *www.compasspointbooks.com*
or e-mail your request to *custserv@compasspointbooks.com*

IMAGE CREDITS

TABLE OF CONTENTS

CHAPTER ONE

BORN OUT OF TAX PROTESTS

We cannot be happy, without being free ... we cannot be free, without being secure in our property ... we cannot be secure in our property, if, without our consent, others may ... take it away.

John Dickinson, *Letters From a Farmer*

On August 14, 1765, shocking news spread through the city of Boston, Massachusetts. A body had been found hanging from a tree on Newbury Street. Closer inspection revealed that the body was not real. It was an effigy, a dummy representing a certain person. The target in this case was Andrew Oliver, a Boston merchant. Oliver had agreed to collect a new tax imposed by the British. A note pinned to the effigy suggested that Oliver had been so ashamed of being a tax collector that he had hanged himself.

The Stamp Act

Bostonians protested a new tax by hanging an effigy of tax collector Andrew Oliver.

Massachusetts was one of Great Britain's 13 American colonies. The people living in the colonies had long thought of themselves as British subjects. They had been content to follow the laws and rules of the king and Parliament, Great Britain's legislature.

This situation began to change in the mid-1760s. A war with France had recently ended. Called the French and Indian War by the colonists, it had lasted from 1754 to 1763.

The British planned to pay the high cost of the French and Indian War by taxing the colonies.

Britain had won the war, but maintaining the territories it had won required thousands of troops. To pay for both the war and the troops, Parliament levied new taxes on the American colonies.

The most unpopular of these taxes were called for by the Stamp Act, passed in 1765. The law taxed paper products, including the paper used to print newspapers, pamphlets, legal and business documents, and even playing cards.

The Loyal Nine

Many colonists were angered by the taxes. Creating the effigy of Andrew Oliver was a form of protest. The British governor, Francis Bernard, understood this, but he intended to punish those who had done it.

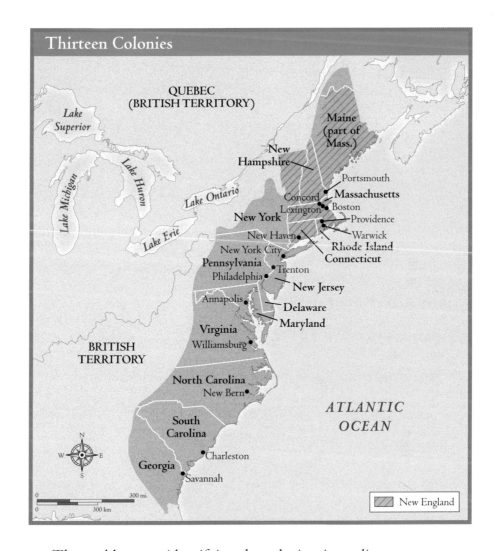

Thirteen Colonies

QUEBEC
(BRITISH TERRITORY)

Lake Superior

Lake Michigan

Lake Huron

Lake Ontario

Lake Erie

Maine
(part of
Mass.)

New
Hampshire

Portsmouth

Concord
Lexington
Boston

Massachusetts

New York

Providence

New Haven
Warwick

New York City
Rhode Island
Connecticut

Pennsylvania
Trenton

Philadelphia
New Jersey

Annapolis
Delaware

Maryland

Virginia

Williamsburg

BRITISH
TERRITORY

North Carolina
New Bern

ATLANTIC
OCEAN

South
Carolina

Charleston

Georgia

Savannah

N
W E
S

0   300 mi.
0   300 km

New England

The problem was identifying the culprits. According to rumor, the effigy was the work of the Loyal Nine. This group of patriotic shopkeepers and artisans met in secret. One of its members was Benjamin Edes, the publisher of a well-known newspaper, the *Boston Gazette*. Edes was upset over the Stamp Act. It forced him to pay hefty new taxes on the paper he used to print his newspaper.

Two other members of the group, Thomas Chase and John Avery, were rum distillers. Their gripe was about an added tax on their licenses to sell liquor. Other members of the Loyal Nine, such as painter Thomas Crafts and jeweler George Trott, had similar complaints.

Around the Liberty Tree

Whether the Loyal Nine made the effigy or incited others to do so remains unclear. What is more certain is that on the day it appeared a crowd gathered on Newbury Street to see it. In the hours that followed, some members of the crowd went on a rampage. They went to Andrew Oliver's tax office and destroyed it. Then they swarmed his home and ransacked it, sending clothes, books, and other belongings flying in all directions. After breaking up Oliver's furniture, they drank his wine cellar dry. British officials tried to stop the destruction, but the rioters pelted them with rocks. Whizzing through the air, these missiles drove the officials away. Other attacks followed in the next two weeks, including one on the home of the lieutenant governor, Thomas Hutchinson.

"THE MOST SAVAGE PEOPLE"

Thomas Hutchinson opposed the Stamp Act. As Massachusetts' lieutenant governor, though, he remained a symbol of the British government. So on August 26, 1765, a mob targeted his Boston home. The governor, Francis Bernard, described the attack in a letter:

> *Being conscious that he had not in the least deserved to be made a party in regard to the Stamp Act, [Hutchinson] rested in full security that the mob would not attack him, and he was at supper with his family when he received advice that the mob were coming to him. He immediately sent away his children, and determined to stay in the house himself, but happily his eldest daughter returned and declared she would not stir from the house unless he went with her; by which means she got him away, which was undoubtedly the occasion of saving his life. For as soon as the mob had got into the house, with a most irresistible fury they immediately looked about for him to murder him. ... They went to work with a rage scarce to be exemplified by the most savage people. Everything movable was destroyed ... except such things of value as were worth carrying off.*

Andrew Oliver became lieutenant governor of Massachusetts in 1771 when his brother-in-law, Thomas Hutchinson, became governor.

After these violent incidents, Andrew Oliver resigned as a tax collector. Celebrations were held across Boston. Many people approved of the protests against what they saw as unfair treatment by the king and Parliament. Some festivities took place around the tree that had held the effigy. It had come to be called the Liberty Tree. As time went on, it became a symbol of the patriots' cause.

In the following years, other trees in the colonies came to be called liberty trees. A South Carolina newspaper reported in 1766 that many merchants and craftsmen had met beneath "a most noble Live Oak Tree in Mr. Mazyck's pasture, which they formally dedicated to Liberty," and had drunk "toasts to their colleagues in Massachusetts."

The Sons of Liberty Emerge

Other staunch protesters joined the Loyal

Nine or formed similar groups. They called

themselves the Sons of Liberty or other

names, such as the Liberty Boys. But colonial loyalists, those who

supported the king and the Stamp Act, called them the Sons of Vio-

lence. Whatever they were called, their motto became "No taxation

without representation!" They meant that as long as no representa-

tive of American colonists could vote in Parliament, it was wrong

for that body to tax the colonies.

People in all of the colonies expressed their opposition to new taxes by protesting in the streets.

Sons of Liberty groups swiftly sprang up in most of the colonies. In just a few months, their ranks numbered at least 2,000. All of them met in secret, but some members were widely known. Besides newspaper publishers such as Edes, Sons of Liberty groups included well-to-do businessmen such as John Hancock and Paul Revere. Popular political figures, including Samuel Adams and his cousin, Massachusetts lawyer and future U.S. president John Adams, also were members.

The Townshend Duties

Eventually protests organized by the Sons of Liberty and other outraged Americans were effective. In March 1766, Parliament repealed the Stamp Act. When news of this reached the colonies, large numbers of colonists celebrated. The sounds of their voices, raised in joyful song, echoed through the streets.

The colonists' joy didn't last long, however. The next year the British launched another moneymaking scheme, the Townshend Duties. Named for British financial officer Charles Townshend, they taxed glass, paints, tea, and other products exported from Britain to the colonies.

Along with many other colonists, the Sons of Liberty protested once again. They helped to distribute the writings of noted Philadelphia lawyer John Dickinson. In his *Letters From a Farmer,* he argued strongly for rejecting the new taxes.

Charles Townshend believed the Townshend Duties would raise money for the British treasury.

"YOU INDEED DESERVE LIBERTY"

In the 12th of his *Letters From a Farmer*, John Dickinson wrote:

Let these truths be indelibly impressed on our minds——that we

cannot be happy without being free——that we cannot be free

without being secure in our property——that we cannot be secure

in our property if without our consent others may, as by right,

take it away——that taxes imposed on us by Parliament do

thus take it away——that duties raised for the sole purpose of

raising money are taxes——that attempts to lay such duties should

be instantly and firmly opposed——that this opposition can never

be effectual unless it is the united effort of these provinces. ...

You will convince the world of the justice of your demands, and

the purity of your intentions. While all mankind must, with

unceasing applauses, confess, that you indeed deserve liberty. ...

For my part, I am resolved strenuously to contend for the liberty

delivered down to me from my ancestors, but whether I shall do

this effectually or not, depends on you, my countrymen.

Spurred on by these words, the Sons of Liberty helped to organize boycotts of the goods taxed by the Townshend Duties. Many Americans refused to drink tea imported from Great Britain, for instance, and they bought only American-made paints and glass.

The efforts were successful. British merchants lost a lot of money. There were rumors that the Townshend Duties would soon be repealed. Patriotic colonists, including the Sons of Liberty, hoped that life would go back to normal. This was not to be. On the day that most of the duties were removed, British soldiers fired on unarmed civilians in Boston. Clearly the colonists' troubles with the mother country were just beginning.

Many colonists spun wool or flax to avoid having to buy it from the British.

CHAPTER TWO

[The British have been] laying every snare that their malevolent [wicked] and corrupt hearts can suggest, to enslave a free people, when this unfortunate country [America] has been striving under many disadvantages ... to preserve their freedom.

New York merchant Alexander McDougall, December 1769

During the three years in which the Townshend Duties were in effect, tensions increased on both sides of the Atlantic. The colonial boycott of British goods caused bitterness in Britain. Meanwhile, letters and petitions condemning the taxes abounded in the colonies. The British responded to the protests with a show of force. They stationed more troops in Boston and other places they viewed as trouble spots. These moves, in turn, led to even more passionate

protests. Violence involving the Sons of

Liberty and other patriots erupted.

British troops armed with muskets entered colonial cities to enforce unpopular laws.

Blood Spills at Golden Hill

One of the most famous of the violent episodes occurred in New

York City in January 1770. It grew out of protests over the upkeep

of British troops in that city. Britain had wanted the colony to pay

for lodging the soldiers. For more than two years, the colony's assem-

bly had taken a patriotic stance and refused to do so. In December

1769, however, the legislators caved in and agreed to pay.

Alexander McDougall served as a general in the Continental Army during the Revolutionary War.

This outraged many New Yorkers, including Alexander McDougall, a merchant and member of the Sons of Liberty. He swiftly wrote a controversial pamphlet that accused the assembly of betraying the people. McDougall boldly used words such as "tyranny" and "enemies" in describing the British and their recent colonial policies.

Angry about McDougall's feisty words, British soldiers retaliated. On January 17, 1770, they sawed down a prominent New York liberty pole. A liberty pole was a tall wooden staff topped by either a patriotic flag or a cone-shaped cap, often called a liberty cap. Like liberty trees, liberty poles were symbols of dissent and freedom. After destroying the pole, the soldiers put up signs that called the Sons of Liberty enemies of society.

BETRAYERS OF LIBERTY'S CAUSE

On December 16, 1769, New York merchant Alexander McDougall published a pamphlet criticizing the colony's assembly. The leaflet said in part:

In a day when the [supporters] of tyranny ... in the mother country and the colonies, are [tireless] in laying every snare that their malevolent and corrupt hearts can suggest, to enslave a free people, when this unfortunate country has been striving under many disadvantages for three years past, to preserve their freedom, [when] the merchants of this city ... have nobly and cheerfully sacrificed their private interest to the public good [by supporting the boycott against the Townshend Duties], it might justly be expected, that [the] representatives of this colony would not be so hardy, nor be so lost to all sense of duty to their [supporters] as to betray the trust committed to them. This they have done in passing the vote to give the [British] troops a thousand pounds out of [the] treasury. ... The liberties of the people are betrayed. In short, they have brought matters to such a pass, that all the checks resulting from the form of our happy constitution are destroyed. ... [You, the people, should protest to the authorities and newspapers] and that you may succeed is the [sincere] desire of A SON OF LIBERTY.

Two days later, another member of the New York Sons of Liberty, Isaac Sears, was unable to control his anger. He and some friends demanded that the soldiers stop hanging signs. When the soldiers refused, Sears and his friends overpowered them. The patriots marched the soldiers, who yelled and cursed them, through the streets toward the town hall. Seeing this, other British troops sounded an alarm. Soon dozens of soldiers and townspeople got into a violent scuffle at Golden Hill, in a rural part of the city. Frightened for their safety, the soldiers brandished their bayonets. They slashed them back and forth in an effort to keep the attackers away. In the chaotic scuffle, several people were wounded and a man was stabbed to death.

Death at the Custom House

News of what happened at Golden Hill spread rapidly through the colonies. Many Americans expressed bitterness and anger over the continued presence of British soldiers in American towns. A few weeks later, the growing tensions led to an even more shocking and violent event in Boston. It is unclear whether any members of the

Several people were injured and one was killed when the Sons of Liberty fought with British soldiers at Golden Hill.

Sons of Liberty were directly involved in the event, which came to be known as the Boston Massacre. But some of the group's leading members used the incident to advance their cause.

Like many New Yorkers, many Bostonians remained troubled over the presence of British soldiers in their streets. The pot of anger and distress finally boiled over. On the evening of March 5, 1770, a British sentry, Private Hugh White, was on guard outside Boston's Custom House. Several young men appeared and began loudly hurling insults at him. Their loud voices could be heard for some distance. Eventually White became upset enough to leave his post. He confronted the men and struck one of them in the side of the head with his musket. In the commotion that followed, a crowd gathered in the now darkened street. Angry people swore at White and threw things at him.

Seeing what was happening, White's superior, Captain Thomas Preston, ordered about a dozen soldiers to go to the private's aid. By the time they arrived, muskets in hand, the crowd had grown to at least 300 people. By now it was too dark for anyone to clearly see what was happening. Apparently, in the gloom, members of the crowd taunted the soldiers and dared them to fire. Suddenly someone in the crowd struck a soldier with a club. Knocked off balance, he fired his weapon. There was a brief, tense pause, during which smoke from the musket drifted through the air. Then the other soldiers fired directly into the crowd. Three colonists were killed. A fourth died a few hours later. A fifth succumbed to his wounds two weeks later.

Hours after the incident, the Sons of Liberty went into action. Samuel Adams labeled it a massacre, a name that stuck. He condemned the soldiers as murderers. He also persuaded another

Tensions had been rising all evening before the Boston Massacre. A crowd grew and became more boisterous until violence erupted.

member of the group, silversmith Paul Revere, to make a detailed engraving of the event. It misleadingly depicts Captain Preston ordering his men to fire on the crowd. Still another Sons of Liberty member, Benjamin Edes, printed the engraving in his newspaper.

Nothing had aroused colonial anger as much as the Boston Massacre. But few people, if anyone, could foresee that Britain's days as America's ruler were numbered.

CAPTAIN PRESTON'S ACCOUNT

An eyewitness account of the Boston Massacre was written by British Captain Thomas Preston:

I saw the people in great commotion, and heard them use the most cruel and horrid threats against the troops. [The mob] surrounded the sentry posted [at the Custom House] and with clubs and other weapons threatened to execute their vengeance on him. I was soon informed by a townsman their intention was to carry off the soldier from his post and probably murder him. ... I immediately sent a non-commissioned officer and 12 men to protect the sentry. ... One of the soldiers, having received a severe blow with a stick, stepped a little on one side and instantly fired, [while] some persons at the same time from behind [called] out, damn your bloods, why don't you fire? Instantly three or four of the soldiers fired, one after another, and directly after three more in the same confusion and hurry. The mob then ran away, except three unhappy men who instantly expired [died].

CHAPTER THREE

DEADLY INFERNO: THE GASPEE AFFAIR

I have long feared that this unhappy contest between Britain and America will end in rivers of blood; should that be the case, America I think may wash her hands in innocence.

Samuel Adams, in a letter concerning the British investigation of the burning of the HMS *Gaspee*

After the Boston Massacre, tensions greatly increased in Britain's North American colonies. More and more, the Sons of Liberty and other patriots viewed the British government as an enemy of freedom. Yet few colonists wanted to break away from the mother country. Even many of the staunchest patriots didn't yet support such a radical step. They simply wanted Parliament and the king to respect their rights as Englishmen. So they were willing to

King George III, who began his rule in 1760, lost the American colonies.

demonstrate their anger and resolve in daring ways. These included acts of protest that most British and loyalists saw as criminal. Just such an act, the first major violent incident after the Boston Massacre, was the *Gaspee* affair.

Attack at Dawn

The HMS *Gaspee* was a small British ship that patrolled the waters off New England. Part of its mission was to help enforce the collection of import and export duties. Its crew inspected the cargo of merchant ships sailed by colonists. This made the *Gaspee* and vessels like it quite unpopular with colonists who viewed British economic policies as unfair.

On June 9, 1772, the *Gaspee* was off the coast of Rhode Island. The captain, William Dudingston, wanted to board a colonial ship and inspect it, but the vessel made a run for it. As it skimmed along the water's surface, the *Gaspee* gave chase. During the pursuit, the *Gaspee* ran aground near Warwick, Rhode Island.

Word of the grounding spread quickly through the nearby communities. That night the members of the Providence chapter of the Sons of Liberty met. They decided to make a bold anti-British political statement by taking advantage of the *Gaspee's* misfortune. At dawn the next day, about 60 members of the Sons of Liberty launched an assault on the stranded ship. Dudingston later described the raiders' approach: "His Majesty's schooner was lying upon a [sandbar]. The sentinels discovered a number of boats coming down the river toward us. … I came up on deck and hailed the boats, forbidding them to come near the schooner, or I should order them to be fired upon. They [ignored the warning] and rowed as fast as they could towards the vessel's bow. I was then using every means in my power to get the guns to bear upon them."

The attackers were led by an experienced naval commander, Abraham Whipple, and a well-known Providence merchant, John Brown. They and other Sons of Liberty quickly seized control of the *Gaspee*. After removing Dudingston and his crew, they torched the ship. The blaze, which sent tall flickering tongues of fire skyward, rapidly turned into a

Abraham Whipple, who was born in Providence, Rhode Island, in 1733, became a captain in the Continental navy.

deadly inferno. It demolished every part of the vessel above the waterline.

The burning of the *Gaspee* brought the colonies one step closer to the Revolutionary War.

To Find and Punish the Perpetrators

Hearing about the capture and burning of the *Gaspee*, the British were outraged. The governor of Rhode Island, Joseph Wanton, offered a reward for information leading to the capture of the attackers. In Britain King George III offered a similar reward. It shows the patriots' loyalty to both their cause and one another that no one tried to collect the rewards.

"SHE WAS ON FIRE"

William Dudingston, captain of the *Gaspee*, later wrote an account of the incident:

> As I was standing myself to oppose [the attackers], and making
> a stroke with my sword ... at that instant I found myself disabled
> in my left arm and shot through the groin. I then stepped from the
> gunwale [and told] them I was mortally wounded. They damned
> me and said I was not wounded; if I was, my own people had done
> it. As loss of blood made me drop upon deck, they ordered me to beg
> [for] my life and commanded the [crew] to surrender. As I saw
> there was no possibility of defending the vessel against such numbers,
> who were in every respect armed and commanded with regularity
> ... I thought it best for the [crew's] preservation to propose to them
> that I would order them to surrender if they assured me [my crew]
> should not be hurt, which they did. ... As I was unable to stand, they
> unbound five of the [crew]men and gave them a blanket to carry me
> up. When I was half way on shore I heard some of the schooner's
> guns go off and heard the [crew] say she [the Gaspee] was on fire.

The king also called for an official investigation of the incident. He formed the Royal Commission of Inquiry. Its task was to find out who had destroyed the *Gaspee* so they could be charged with treason and taken to Britain to stand trial. King George told the commissioners: "You are to use your utmost care and diligence ... in making a very full and particular inquiry into all the circumstances relative to the attacking, plundering, and burning [of] our armed schooner the *Gaspee*, on the tenth of June last in the Narragansett river, within our said Colony of Rhode Island, and [why and how it happened], for the discovery and punishment of

The wanted poster issued for the capture of those responsible for burning the *Gaspee* yielded nothing.

By the Honorable JOSEPH WANTON, Esquire, Governor, Captain General, and Commander in Chief, of and over the English Colony of Rhode-Island, and Providence Plantations, in New-England, in America.

(L. S.)

A PROCLAMATION.

WHEREAS on *Tuesday*, the ninth Instant in the Night, a Number of People, unknown, boarded His Majesty's armed Schooner the *Gaspee*, as she lay aground on a Point of Land, called *Nanquit*, a little to the southward of *Pawtuxet*, in the Colony aforesaid, who dangerously wounded Lieutenant *William Duddingston* the Commander, and by Force took him with all his People, put them into Boats, and landed them near *Pawtuxet*; and afterwards set Fire to the said Schooner, whereby she was entirely destroyed:

I HAVE, therefore, thought fit, by and with the Advice of such of His Majesty's Council, as could be seasonably convened, to issue this Proclamation, strictly charging and commanding all His Majesty's Officers within the said Colony, both Civil and Military, to exert themselves with the utmost Vigilance, to discover and apprehend the Persons guilty of the aforesaid atrocious Crime, that they may be brought to condign Punishment. And I do hereby offer a Reward of ONE HUNDRED POUNDS, Sterling Money of Great-Britain, to any Person or Persons who shall discover the Perpetrators of the said Villainy, to be paid immediately upon the Conviction of any one or more of them.

AND the several Sheriffs in the said Colony are hereby required, forthwith, to cause this Proclamation to be posted up in the most public Places, in each of the Towns in their respective Counties.

GIVEN under my Hand and Seal at Arms, at Newport, this Twelfth Day of June, in the Twelfth Year of the Reign of His Most Sacred Majesty, GEORGE THE THIRD, by the Grace of God, King of Great-Britain, and so forth, Annoq; Dom. One Thousand, Seven Hundred and Seventy-two.

J. WANTON.

By his Honor's Command,
HENRY WARD, Sec'ry.

GOD SAVE THE KING.

the perpetrators of those heinous [terrible] offenses."

Along with many other colonists, the Sons of Liberty were angry about the British actions. In particular they found the idea of putting colonists on trial in faraway Britain to be insulting and unacceptable. Samuel Adams, now a leader of the Sons of Liberty, repeatedly criticized the commission. It had been given almost tyrannical authority, he said. The investigators aimed to trample on the colonists' cherished right, as Englishmen, to be tried by their peers, Adams said. He insisted that any such trial take place in the American colonies.

A graduate of Harvard College, Samuel Adams was a businessman and tax collector before he decided to become a politician.

THE GLORIOUS CAUSE OF FREEDOM

In the months following the *Gaspee* incident, Samuel Adams wrote letters condemning the British investigation of the ship's destruction. This one was printed in the *Providence Gazette* on December 26, 1772:

A court of inquisition, more horrid than that of Spain or Portugal, is established within this colony, to inquire into the circumstances of destroying the Gaspee schooner; and the persons who are the commissioners of this new-fangled court, are vested with [the] most [excessive] and unconstitutional power. They are directed to summon witnesses, apprehend persons [and] deliver them to Admiral Montagu, who is ordered to have a ship in readiness to carry them to England, where they are to be tried. ... Who among the natives of America can hear it without emotion? Is there an American, in whose breast there glows the smallest spark of public virtue, but who must be fired with indignation and resentment against a measure so replete with the ruin of our free constitution? To be tried by one's peers is the greatest privilege a subject can wish for, [and] the tools of despotism and arbitrary power, have long wished that this important [safeguard] might be destroyed. ... My countrymen, it [is your] duty to stand forth in the glorious cause of freedom, the dearest of all your earthly enjoyments; and, with a truly Roman spirit of liberty, either prevent the fastening of the infernal chains now forging for you, and your posterity, or nobly perish in the attempt.

A Disturbing Realization

Many Americans agreed with Adams' sentiments. Some, like him, spoke out publicly against what they thought were continuing British abuses. In Boston, for instance, a minister named John Allen delivered a sermon on the *Gaspee* affair and its aftermath. Standing before his congregation, he sternly denounced the royal commission and the plan to ship accused colonists across the ocean for trial. The sermon was printed and reprinted several times. It became one of the most widely read pamphlets in the years just before the Revolutionary War.

The large-scale investigation of the *Gaspee's* destruction turned out to be a serious mistake by the British. It kept the incident alive in the colonial press for a long time. It also awakened many colonists to a disturbing realization: Sooner or later, to get their full rights as Englishmen, they might have to fight the mother country.

CHAPTER FOUR

OF TEA, TAR, AND FEATHERS

The People should never rise [rebel], without doing something to be remembered—something notable and striking. This destruction of the tea is so bold, so daring, so firm, [and] intrepid [that] it must [have] important consequences.

From the diary of American patriot, and future president, John Adams, written the day after the Boston Tea Party

After the *Gaspee* incident, the Sons of Liberty kept resisting British authority. In an even more daring exploit, late in 1773, they staged the Boston Tea Party. The term *party* was a play on words. The episode was really a major destruction of property intended to send a message to the British government; it was hardly a *party* to the British.

The Tea Act

The chain of events leading to the Boston Tea Party began with the Townshend Duties. Most had been repealed by 1770. But a few remained in effect, the most notable being a tax on tea imported from Great Britain. For a while, this didn't cause a problem for most colonists. They boycotted tea imported from England, refusing to buy or drink it. Sooner or later, they reasoned, the British would give up on the tea tax.

They didn't. British merchants

Talk of taxes imposed by the British always got the crowd riled up at Sons of Liberty meetings.

and lawmakers kept trying to increase revenues from tea. In May 1773, Parliament passed the Tea Act. It allowed the British East India Company to sell its tea to the North American colonies at an unusually low price. Some colonists saw this move in a positive light because it made tea less expensive.

Other patriots, including the Sons of Liberty, opposed the Tea Act. In their

The British East India Company traded many items, including tea, silk, and cotton, that were important for everyday life.

view, it was just a ploy to get colonists to buy British tea again and ruin the boycott. Samuel Adams urged local agents of the British East India Company to ignore the law. The agents who didn't heed his words were terrorized. Members of the Sons of Liberty ransacked their places of business and homes. Adams also organized protest meetings that were attended by thousands of people. Once more angry shouts echoed through the streets as they denounced both the Tea Act and the British government.

Into the Harbor

In yet another form of protest, patriots tried to block the unloading of tea. The major ports where British tea entered the colonies were New York, Philadelphia, Charleston, and Boston. In these cities, patriots warned captains of ships carrying British tea not to unload it. The captains were told to sail away or face unpleasant consequences. Out of fear, many of the captains sailed out of the harbor.

In Boston, however, Thomas Hutchinson, who had become the royal governor in 1771, stepped in. He made sure the ships carrying tea stayed in the harbor. Upset over this move, the local

Sons of Liberty sprang into action. On December 16, 1773, many

members of the group dressed as Indians and headed for Grif-

fin's wharf. There three British ships loaded with tea—the HMS

Dartmouth, HMS *Beaver*, and HMS *Elea-*

nor—were docked. One of the disguised

patriots, shoemaker George Hewes, later

Governor Thomas Hutchinson refused to allow the tea on ships docked in Boston to be returned to Great Britain.

recalled: "It was now evening, and I immediately dressed myself in the costume of an Indian, equipped with a small hatchet [and] a club. After having painted my face and hands with coal dust in the shop of a blacksmith, I repaired to Griffin's wharf. ... When I first appeared in the street after being thus disguised, I fell in with many who were dressed, equipped and painted as I was."

The men divided into three groups, and each group boarded one of the ships. In just a few hours they managed to dump 342 containers of tea, which splashed into Boston Harbor and sank. According to Hewes: "In about three hours from the time we went on board, we had thus broken and thrown overboard every tea chest to be found in the ship, while those in the other ships were disposing of the tea in the same way, at the same time. We were surrounded by British armed ships, but no attempt was made to resist us."

The Sons of Liberty dumped the tea to make a political point. Under no circumstances did they want to give the impression that they were trying to steal the tea for their own use.

DEALING WITH TEA THIEVES

During the Boston Tea Party, some Bostonians tried to steal some of the tea. A member of the Sons of Liberty, George Hewes, later recalled:

During the time we were throwing the tea overboard, there were several attempts made by some of the citizens of Boston ... to carry off small quantities of it for their family use. To effect that object, they would watch their opportunity to snatch up a handful from the deck [and] put it into their pockets. One Captain O'Connor, whom I well knew, came on board for that purpose, and when he supposed he was not noticed, filled his pockets. ... But I had detected him and gave information to the captain of what he was doing. We [took] him into custody. ... Another attempt was made to save a little tea from the ruins of the cargo by a tall, aged man who wore a large cocked hat and white wig, which was fashionable at that time. He had [artfully] slipped a little into his pocket, but being detected, they seized him and, taking his hat and wig from his head, threw them, together with the tea [in] his pockets, into the water. In consideration of his advanced age, he was permitted to escape.

The Colonists Divided

Reactions to the Boston Tea Party were predictable. Patriotic colonists, including John Adams, applauded it. But most British and colonial loyalists were outraged. They saw the destruction of the tea as a criminal act and called for those who did it to be punished. The residents of nearly every colonial town and city were divided over the issue. In the months after the incident, bad feelings sometimes led to insults and even physical assaults.

The most disturbing and widely publicized of the attacks involved John Malcolm. He was a loyalist in Boston who worked for the British customs service. Malcolm was angry about

John Adams served as the country's first vice president, under President George Washington, and later as the second president.

the Tea Party. He may have been eager to confront members of the Sons of Liberty who had taken part in the event.

On January 25, 1774, only a few weeks after the Boston Tea Party, Malcolm got into a street fight with George Hewes, a patriot who had dumped tea into the harbor. Malcolm struck Hewes with a stick. Blood gushed from a gash in the injured man's forehead. Hewes was treated by Doctor Joseph Warren, another member of the Sons of Liberty. That evening several other members dragged Malcolm from his house. They tarred and feathered him, a painful and humiliating form of punishment. First they poured hot tar over his body. Then they applied feathers, which stuck to the tar that coated the screaming man.

Incidents like Malcolm's tarring and feathering sometimes gave the Sons of Liberty a bad name. Many colonists still saw them as heroic fighters for freedom and civil rights. But others disapproved of their most violent tactics and saw them as criminals.

The members of the group itself didn't always agree about tactics. George Hewes felt that tarring and feathering was barbaric. Despite his differences with Malcolm, he tried to stop his fellow

Sons of Liberty. Hewes tried to throw a blanket over the man to end his humiliation. But the others shoved him aside and continued the punishment. Some people saw it as a sign of things to come. They worried that the colonies' differences with the mother country could no longer be settled peacefully. They were right.

MALCOLM'S ORDEAL

An eyewitness described John Malcolm's painful,
frightening ordeal:

> *They proceeded to elevate Mr. Malcolm from his sled into a cart,*
> *and stripping him to buff and breaches [to his underwear], gave*
> *him a [tarring and feathering] and [dragged] him away to a*
> *liberty tree, where they [ordered] him to renounce [give up] his*
> *present commission [job helping the British] and swear that he*
> *would never hold another [job] inconsistent with the liberties*
> *of his country. But this he [stubbornly] refused [to do, and]*
> *they then carted him to the gallows [platform where criminals*
> *were hanged], passed a rope round his neck, and threw the other*
> *end over the beam, as if they intended to hang him. But [he still*
> *remained defiant]. They then ... threatened to cut his ears off,*
> *and on this he complied [agreed to their demands], and they then*
> *brought him home.*

CHAPTER FIVE

THE SHOT HEARD 'ROUND THE WORLD

[Now] is the time when all should be united in opposition to this violation of the liberties of all.

Excerpt from a letter to the public written by Boston patriots dismayed over Britain's imposition of the Coercive Acts in 1774

The Boston Tea Party had been the boldest move yet made by the Sons of Liberty and other American patriots. They had hoped to get the full attention of British leaders and lawmakers. They certainly did. The question now was how the British would react. As John Adams put it: "What measures will the [British] take in consequence of this? Will they resent it? Will they dare to resent it? Will they punish us? [And if so,] how?"

The Coercive Acts

The answers to these questions were not long in coming. In March and June 1774, Parliament passed the Coercive Acts. They were designed, in part, to punish Boston. But they were also intended to force the American colonists to bend to the will of the king and Parliament.

The colonists had a different name for the new laws: the Intolerable Acts. They viewed them as unfair and unbearable. One law shut down Boston's port until the local

Act for blocking up the Harbour of *Boston*.

The Boston Port Act was one British response to the Boston Tea Party.

residents paid for the lost tea. Another law put limits on Massachusetts' assembly, making it almost powerless. In addition, colonists were required to let British soldiers stay in their homes.

Many patriots, from New England to Georgia, took these new laws to heart. They believed that the punishment of Boston was meant in part to intimidate the other colonies into submission.

A new Quartering Act required colonists to allow soldiers to stay in their homes.

SUPPRESSING THE SPIRIT OF LIBERTY

The Sons of Liberty and other patriots in the colonies communicated with one another through letters. The small groups that wrote the letters were called committees of correspondence. In response to the Coercive Acts, the Boston committee sent out an announcement in May 1774:

The town of Boston is treated in a manner the most ignominious [shameful], cruel, and unjust. The Parliament [has] ordered our port to be entirely shut up, leaving us barely so much of the means of subsistence as to keep us from perishing with cold and hunger; and it is said that [a] fleet of British ships of war is to block up our harbor until we shall make restitution to the East India Company for the loss of their tea, which was destroyed therein the winter past. ... This attack, though made immediately upon us, is doubtless designed for every other colony who will not surrender their sacred rights and liberties into the hands of an infamous ministry. ... Their grand object is to divide the colonies. [Be] assured, you will be called upon to surrender your rights if ever they should succeed in their attempts to suppress the spirit of liberty here. The single question then is, whether you consider Boston as now suffering in the common cause, and sensibly feel and resent [this] injury and affront.

But they refused to be intimidated. To demonstrate their support for Boston, nearly all the colonies sent food and other supplies to help its residents.

Another expression of the rising spirit of unity came May 27, 1774. Eighty-nine members of Virginia's legislature—which had been closed down by Lord Dunmore, the last royal governor of Virginia—met in a tavern. Among them were George Washington and Thomas Jefferson. The group boldly declared: "An attack made on one of our sister colonies ... is an attack made on all British America, and threatens ruin to the rights of all, unless the united wisdom of the whole be applied."

The Battles at Lexington and Concord

An even more daring act of colonial solidarity took place a few months later. In September, 56 representatives from 12 of the 13 colonies met in Philadelphia. They called themselves the Continental Congress. They didn't want separation from the mother country. But they demanded fairer treatment and all their rights as British subjects. After Parliament and the king largely ignored

the demands, tensions in the colonies continued to rise.

In this explosive atmosphere, large-scale violence was probably unavoidable. The immediate events leading to the first shots of the Revolutionary War took place in April 1775. Massachusetts' new governor, General Thomas Gage, heard that some patriots in the colony had been collecting weapons. The weapons were stored in Concord, a village several miles west of Boston. Gage ordered officers to take about 700 soldiers, go to Concord, and seize the weapons. The Sons of Liberty heard what was happening. Some of them rode to Concord to warn the citizens of the approaching British.

The warnings stirred the colonists into action. When the British reached Lexington on the morning of April 19 on their way to Concord, they found about 70 armed patriots waiting for them in the town square. Soon shots rang out and musket smoke filled the air. Who first fired remains uncertain. Eight colonists died in the bloody skirmish. The British redcoats moved on to Concord, where another small battle was fought. Then the British officer in charge received alarming news: Thousands of armed colonists were moving toward Concord from all directions. Seeing no choice, he ordered his men to retreat. On the way back to Boston, patriots repeatedly ambushed the marching soldiers. As the snipers' musket balls flew, redcoat after redcoat collapsed into the dust. At the end of the day, British losses totaled 73 dead, 174 wounded, and 26 missing.

Down the Corridors of History

The battles at Lexington and Concord didn't just signal the start of a war between the colonies and Britain. The effects of those first shots would be felt around the world. This is because the colonies went on to win the conflict. Separating from the mother country, they became a new nation—the United States of America.

The Battle of Concord Bridge was one of the first battles in the eight-year war.

This country's democratic institutions and respect for human rights became models for people seeking freedom across the globe. The Sons of Liberty played a key role in making these things happen. Their deeds also inspired others in later struggles for liberty.

All of these things were predicted by colonial patriot Jacob Green of New Jersey. His words, in a pamphlet read by

The Sons of Liberty played a large role in the colonies' fight for freedom from Great Britain.

many colonists, would later echo with the ring of truth down the corridors of history:

If we are independent, this land of liberty will be glorious on many accounts. Population will abundantly increase, agriculture will be promoted, trade will flourish, religion, unrestrained by human laws, will have free course to run and prevail, and America [will] be an asylum [refuge] for all noble spirits and sons of liberty from all parts of the world. ... Here they may expand and [triumph]; here they may enjoy all the blessings which [the earth] can afford to fallen men.

TIMELINE

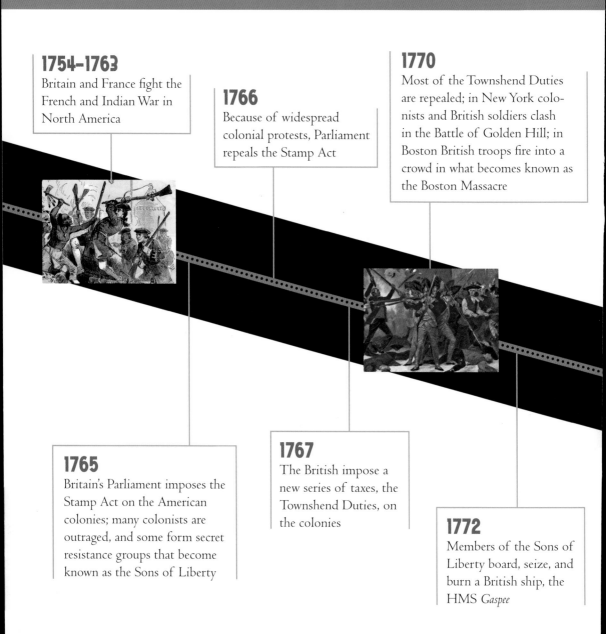

1754–1763
Britain and France fight the French and Indian War in North America

1766
Because of widespread colonial protests, Parliament repeals the Stamp Act

1770
Most of the Townshend Duties are repealed; in New York colonists and British soldiers clash in the Battle of Golden Hill; in Boston British troops fire into a crowd in what becomes known as the Boston Massacre

1765
Britain's Parliament imposes the Stamp Act on the American colonies; many colonists are outraged, and some form secret resistance groups that become known as the Sons of Liberty

1767
The British impose a new series of taxes, the Townshend Duties, on the colonies

1772
Members of the Sons of Liberty board, seize, and burn a British ship, the HMS *Gaspee*

1773

As a protest, Sons of Liberty members dressed as Indians board British ships in Boston Harbor and throw tons of tea overboard, an incident that comes to be called the Boston Tea Party

1775

The first shots of the Revolutionary War ring out as colonists and British soldiers clash in the Massachusetts villages of Lexington and Concord

1783

The Americans and British sign a peace treaty, and the war ends

1774

In retaliation for the Boston Tea Party, Parliament imposes the Coercive Acts, which the colonists call the Intolerable Acts

1776

The American colonies declare their independence from Britain, becoming a new nation, the United States of America

GLOSSARY

artisan: craftsperson or other skilled manual worker

boycotts: refusals to do business with certain businesses as a form of protest

controversial: causing disagreement

duties: taxes on imported or exported goods

effigy: crude dummy representing a hated person

engraving: picture made by carving or etching on a flat surface

humiliating: extremely embarrassing

inferno: intense, destructive fire

legislature: group of elected or appointed persons who gather to make laws

liberty pole: wooden pole, topped by a flag or cap, symbolizing freedom

liberty tree: tree symbolizing freedom

loyalist: colonist who remained faithful to the king and Parliament at the time of the American Revolution

Parliament: Britain's national legislature

peer: member of one's own group or community

perpetrator: someone who commits a certain act, often a crime

repeal: cancel

schooner: small sailing ship

sentinel: guard

ADDITIONAL RESOURCES

Further Reading

Burgan, Michael. *The Boston Massacre.* Minneapolis: Compass Point Books, 2005.

Burgan, Michael. *The Boston Tea Party.* Minneapolis: Compass Point Books, 2001.

Irvin, Benjamin. *Samuel Adams: Son of Liberty, Father of Revolution.* New York: Oxford University Press, 2002.

Kjelle, Marylou Morano. *The Life and Times of John Hancock.* Hockessin, Del.: Mitchell Lane Publishers, 2007.

Murray, Stuart. *American Revolution.* New York: DK Publishing, 2005.

Nardo, Don. *The American Revolution.* San Diego: KidHaven Press, 2002.

Poe, Marshall. *Sons of Liberty.* New York: Aladdin Paperbacks, 2008.

Raatma, Lucia. *The Battles of Lexington and Concord.* Minneapolis: Compass Point Books, 2004.

Internet Sites

FactHound offers a safe, fun way to find Internet sites related to this book. All of the sites on FactHound have been researched by our staff.

Here's all you do:
   Visit *www.facthound.com*
FactHound will fetch the best sites for you.

Look for more *Taking a Stand* books:

Freedom Fighter: William Wallace and Scotland's Battle for Independence

Refusing to Crumble: The Danish Resistance in World War II

Striking Back: The Fight to End Child Labor Exploitation

SELECT BIBLIOGRAPHY

Commager, Henry Steele, and Richard B. Morris, eds. *The Spirit of 'Seventy-Six: The Story of the American Revolution as Told by Participants.* New York: Da Capo Press, 2002.

Countryman, Edward. *The American Revolution.* New York: Hill and Wang, 2003.

Dann, John C., ed. *The Revolution Remembered: Eyewitness Accounts of the War for Independence.* Chicago: University of Chicago Press, 1983.

Dudley, William, ed. *The American Revolution: Opposing Viewpoints.* San Diego: Greenhaven Press, 1992.

Fischer, David Hackett. *Liberty and Freedom.* New York: Oxford University Press, 2005.

Fischer, David Hackett. *Paul Revere's Ride.* New York: Oxford University Press, 1994.

Jensen, Merrill. *The Founding of a Nation: A History of the American Revolution, 1763–1776.* Indianapolis: Hackett Publishing Company, 2004.

Morgan, Edmund S. *The Birth of the Republic, 1763–89.* Chicago: University of Chicago Press, 1992.

Morgan, Edmund S., and Helen M. Morgan. *The Stamp Act Crisis: Prologue to Revolution.* Chapel Hill: University of North Carolina Press, 1995.

Unger, Harlow G. *John Hancock: Merchant King and American Patriot.* New York: John Wiley & Sons, 2000.

Ward, Harry M. *The American Revolution: Nationhood Achieved, 1763–1788.* New York: St. Martin's Press, 1995.

Wood, Gordon S. *The Radicalism of the American Revolution.* New York: Vintage Books, 1993.

SOURCE NOTES

Chapter 1: John Dickinson. *Letters from a Farmer in Pennsylvania.* 4 Sept. 2009. http://oll. libertyfund.org/index.php?option=com_staticxt&staticfile=show.php%3Ftitle=690&l ayout=html#chapter_102311

William Dudley, ed. *The American Revolution: Opposing Viewpoints.* San Diego: Greenhaven Press, 1992, p. 44.

Chaper 2: Alexander McDougall. "To the Betrayed Inhabitants of the City and Colony of New York." 4 Sept. 2009. http://academic.brooklyn.cuny.edu/history/burrows/ AmRev/Documents/McDougall.htm

"Captain Thomas Preston's Account of the Boston Massacre." From Revolution to Reconstruction. 4 Sept. 2009. http://odur.let.rug.nl/~usa/D/1751-1775/boston-massacre/prest.htm

Chapter 3: "Correspondence to and from Samuel Adams on the *Gaspee* Incident." Gaspee Virtual Archives. 4 Sept. 2009. http://gaspee.org/SamAdams.html#Sessions_ to_Adams25Dec1772

"Lieutenant Dudingston's Report on the Burning of the *Gaspee*." Gaspee Virtual Archives. 4 Sept. 2009. http://www.gaspee.org/StaplesGaspee.htm

"King George III's Instructions to the *Gaspee* Commissioners." Gaspee Virtual Archives. 4 Sept. 2009. http://gaspee.org/KingGeorgeInstructions.htm

Chapter 4: Adams Family Papers. "Diary, 16 December 1772–18 December 1773." The Massachusetts Historical Society. 4 Sept. 2009. www.masshist.org/digitaladams/ aea/cfm/doc.cfm?id=D19

"Boston Tea Party: Eyewitness Account by a Participant." The History Place. 4 Sept. 2009. www.historyplace.com/unitedstates/revolution/teaparty.htm

Alfred F. Young. *The Shoemaker and the Tea Party: Memory and the American Revolution.* Boston: Beacon Press, 2000, pp. 49–50.

Chapter 5: "Circular Letter of the Boston Committee of Correspondence; May 13, 1774." Yale Law School. 4 Sept. 2009. http://avalon.law.yale.edu/18th_century/ circ_let_boston_1774.asp

William Dudley, ed. *The American Revolution: Opposing Viewpoints.* San Diego: Greenhaven Press, 1992, p. 146.

INDEX

ABOUT THE AUTHOR

Historian and award-winning author Don Nardo has written many books for young people about American history, including *The Battle of Saratoga* for Compass Point Books. Nardo lives with his wife, Christine, in Massachusetts.